creating**outdoor**rooms

creating**outdoor**rooms

Leeda Marting
Photography by Terry Richardson

Gibbs Smith, Publisher
TO ENRICH AND INSPIRE HUMANKIND
Charleston | Santa Fe | Santa Barbara

First Edition
11 10 09 08 07 5 4 3 2 1

Published by
Gibbs Smith, Publisher
P.O. Box 667
Layton, Utah 84041

Orders: 1.800.835.4993
www.gibbs-smith.com

Designed by Debra McQuiston
Printed and bound in China

Library of Congress Cataloging-in-Publication Data

Marting, Leeda.
  Creating outdoor rooms / Leeda Marting ; photographs by
Terry Richardson. — 1st ed.
    p. cm.
  ISBN-13: 978-0-941711-99-9
  ISBN-10: 0-941711-99-4
  1. Garden rooms. 2. Garden ornaments and furniture.
3. Landscape gardening. I. Title.

SB473.M2956 2007
643'.55—dc22

2007011271

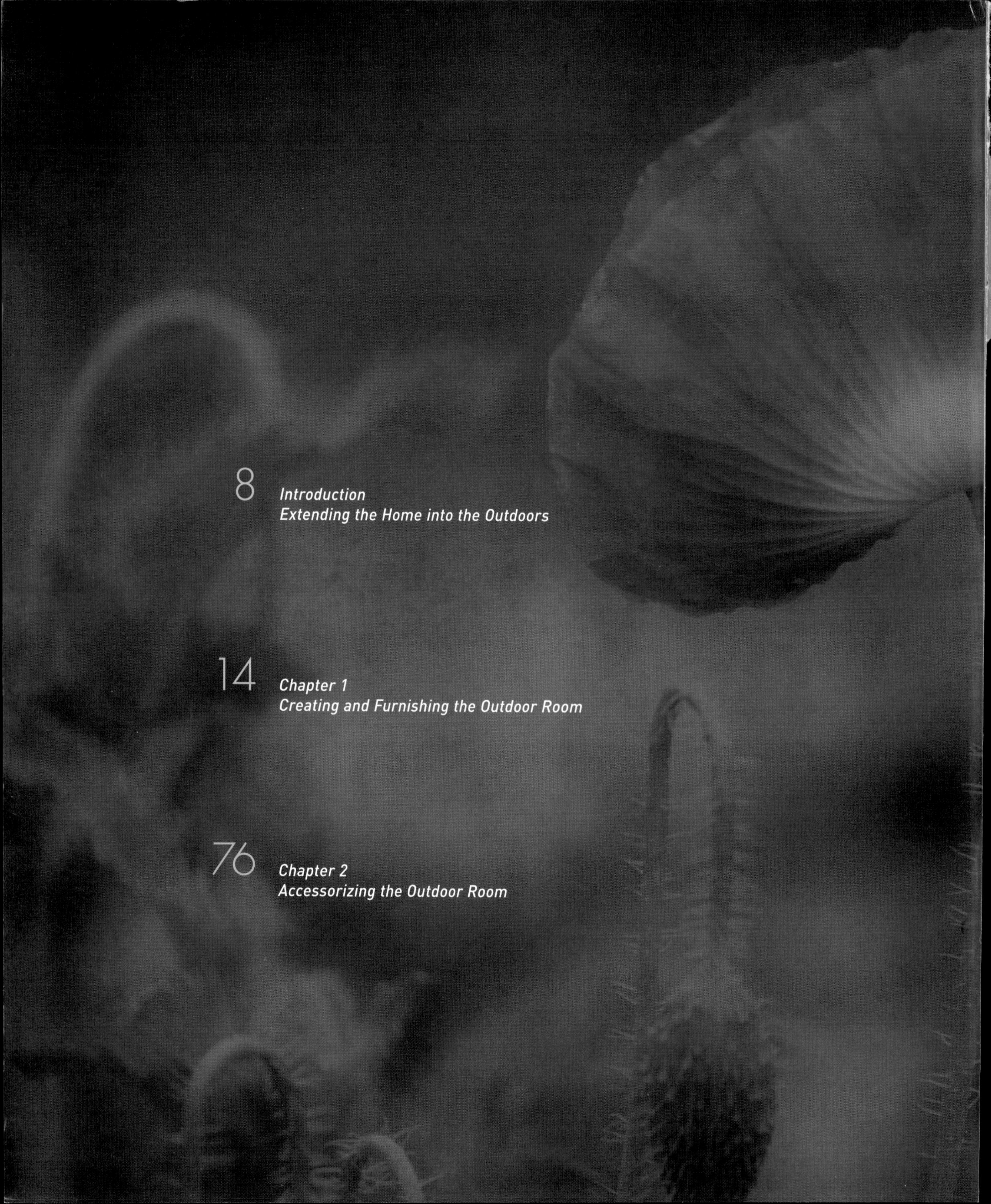

Extending the Home into the Outdoors

Though outdoor rooms most likely had their beginning as early as the first settlements in Mesopotamia, a compelling case can be made that outdoor rooms in the United States began in Charleston, one of our nation's oldest cities and a city with a rich horticultural history.

Modeled after European cities, where houses were built close together, Charleston's city plan called for long and narrow lots that resulted in rectangular houses with the gable facing the street. The Charleston single house, as it is known, has its porch, or "piazza," constructed perpendicular to the street, along the length of the south or west side of the house. The piazza—an outdoor room—is just a door opening away from the interior of the house and extends family and social life outside.

Unlike houses with a front porch that faces the street, the Charleston single house's porch, or piazza, looks out to a garden. Walls most often enclose the garden, resulting in extended living space, with areas for play, dining, congenial conversation or quiet contemplation.

Today, most American homes have porches, decks or lanais to the rear of the house that may face a garden or pool area. Whatever the configuration of the house, outdoor rooms are a way of gaining living space while enjoying nature.

The popularity of outdoor rooms today is based on a number of factors, including our love of the outdoor lifestyle. Beginning in 2000, a housing boom—driven by low-interest mortgages—enabled many people to become homeowners. The baby boomers invested in better housing, which included outdoor rooms equipped with fireplaces, kitchens, pools and other amenities. Home as sanctuary—in the post-9/11 era—has also played a role in the homeowners' desire for beautiful gardens and places within them for outdoor living.

Outdoor rooms in Charleston, and their growth elsewhere, share these characteristics:

Outdoor rooms are not defined by space alone. Inside the home, four walls define a room. In historic Charleston, stucco or brick walls were constructed around the garden for privacy and protection. Walls, gates, hedges and other devices defined the boundaries of an outdoor room while providing sanctuary from the outside world and a relatively worry-free oasis for children and pets.

Today, an outdoor room is as much a state of mind as it is a space. It can be defined by a simple

row of boxwoods or the curve of a planting bed. It may be a porch, a poolside conversation area, or a terrace twenty stories high in an urban setting. It is anyplace that allows us to connect to the restorative power of nature.

Outdoor rooms are intimate. Charleston's courtyard gardens are often small with lower maintenance requirements. The limited space, however, is utilized to its maximum. Even where larger parcels of land exist, the space is broken down into smaller and more intimate areas. Today's condominium and town house home-owners have elected a lifestyle that encompasses downsized space characterized by maximized use. In brief, outdoor rooms are in; colossal land-scapes are out.

Free movement exists between the home and outside, with the garden room as essential as the rooms inside. Charlestonians cannot imagine a home without a garden room. They personalize their outdoor space in the same manner and with as much care as any interior room. They cook and dine indoors and outside. Seating arrangements

for conversation are important indoors as well as on the piazza or in the garden. An afternoon snooze may be taken on a chaise longue near the pool or on the living room sofa. Movement natu-rally takes place between inside and outside, limited by only one factor: inclement weather.

Furnishings and accessories are skillfully combined for beauty, comfort and pleasure. It is hard to imagine a Charleston outdoor room with-out comfortable seating for conversation or dining, a bubbling water feature, pots overflowing with flowers, a birdhouse nearby, and other acces-sories that bring pleasure and warmth to outdoor living.

In the pages that follow, we will explore the creation of outdoor or garden rooms. This book is about making life outside as comfortable and enjoyable as life indoors, building upon the tradi-tions and style found in the great historic homes and gardens of Charleston, where outdoor rooms began. All of the photography shown on these pages was taken in Charleston.

Indoor comfort is now available in outdoor furniture, with the same stylish good looks of interior décor.

With today's wide range of outdoor furniture materials and styles, aesthetics need not be sacrificed for functionality.

Glass tops are better suited to covered areas (rather than direct outdoor use) and add a more formal touch to the table.

Due to its versatility, aluminum may be the most important material used for outdoor furniture today.

Wrought iron became popular in outdoor furniture because of its look, its durability and its ability to resist the wind due to its weight.

Unless painted or stained, these weather- and rot-resistant woods will age to a silvery gray.

CHAPTER 1

Creating and Furnishing the Outdoor Room

Nature lures us outdoors to the sunshine, fresh air, lush greenery and the sound of birds. We love the peace and tranquility of the garden. Comfortable furniture permits us to enjoy the outdoors as a place for lively conversation with friends or as a respite for quiet reading or a nap. The options for outdoor furnishings are as numerous as those inside the home.

Tranquility and Comfort

Bringing the beauty of the outdoors inside is usually done with plants or cut flowers. By using man-made materials, the home can be extended outside, where the latter becomes like all the rooms in the house—stylish, inviting and comfortable.

Creating the Outdoor Room

The first step in creating an outdoor room is to look inside the house. An outdoor room should complement and extend the home, and not be a bold departure from the style of the interior furnishings or the architectural design of the structure.

The location of an outdoor room may be obvious if a piazza, porch or terrace is already attached. If no such space exists, seek those areas where doors lead out, or create an opening to a favorable location. Accessibility is key to using an outdoor room. Space permitting, there can be more than one room outside.

The size of an outdoor room is dictated by its use and the space available. If entertaining is high on the agenda, the size needs to accommodate both dining and seating areas. Or separate the two functions into two different outdoor rooms, just as the living and dining rooms may be separate inside. If a tranquil retreat for quiet work is what you have in mind, a small area may suffice.

Many outdoor rooms today have fireplaces, built-in kitchens, and other amenities that add to the quality of life and the value of the home. Simple improvements outside, however, can create charming outdoor rooms that are affordable for most households.

Furnishing the Outdoor Room

Over the past decade, a revolution has taken place in outdoor furnishings. Indoor comfort is now available in outdoor furniture, with the same stylish good looks of interior décor. Where once the fabric options were limited, today's outdoor fabrics are virtually indistinguishable from those

used in the living room. They look good, feel good and come in an almost unlimited colorfast pallet. The availability of stylish all-weather furnishings has been one of the major factors in the popularity of garden rooms.

Choose outdoor furniture that complements the architecture and interior furnishings of the house. The styles, colors and fabrics used outside should all be extensions of the home, never compromising quality. If there are fine furnishings inside, it makes little sense not to invest outside as well.

Decide what you want in your outdoor experience. With today's wide range of outdoor furniture materials and styles, aesthetics need not be sacrificed for functionality. Outdoor furniture can be both beautiful and comfortable. Consider how you plan to use your time outdoors. Do you want

comfortable seating for conversation? Poolside chaises for sunbathing? Bar-height tables and stools for convivial gatherings? Portable dining options for flexible entertaining? A wide lounge chair that will accommodate you and your child or pet?

Look for good workmanship and design. For example, if the furniture is made of wood, look for sanding smooth to the touch and mortise-and-tenon joints with no gaps. Does the furniture sit firmly on a surface? Are the shape, proportion and lines of the piece pleasing to the eye?

Consider your local weather. Wood furniture will tend to mildew if exposed to prolonged rain periods. Though aluminum furniture with a powder coat finish functions well in snow or rain, it may not endure the seaside's salt air and strong sun. Synthetic materials are best in coastal settings.

Classic Designs in Modern Materials

Until the industrial revolution and the advent of iron, garden furniture was limited chiefly to stone and wood. One can imagine a host pulling his precious Chippendale mahogany chair from the dining room and placing it on the piazza as extra seating when

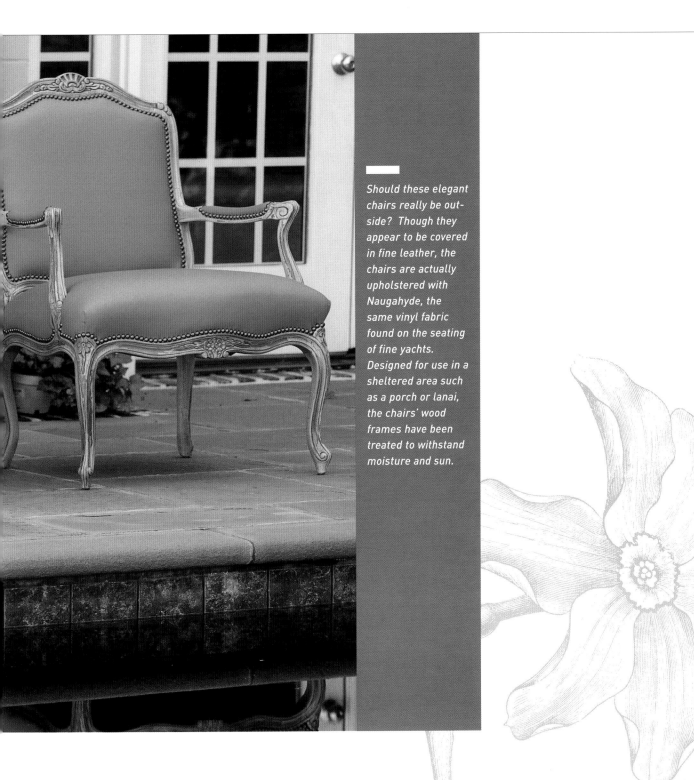

guests arrived. Indoor comfort, thanks to the new technology, is now available outdoors in durable weatherproof furniture.

It should come as no surprise that some of the finest outdoor furniture today is based on classic designs from the past: Sheraton, Chippendale, Windsor, Hepplewhite, Louis XV, and others. However, while the designs may resemble wood furniture, the materials are quite different and are engineered to withstand harsh weather conditions.

FACING: *In the late eighteenth century, the elegant Sheraton design was introduced. Interpreted today in cast aluminum, the outdoor chair includes the now-familiar, comfortable shield back. The seat cushion is covered in a sun- and mildew-resistant fabric.*

LEFT: *The twentieth century ushered in the era of modern design. This handsome armchair with simple lines is made of aluminum and all-weather woven wicker. It will stand up to the elements while providing style and comfort.*

FACING LEFT: *The design of this handsome chair is evocative of the Napoleonic period. Crafted of aluminum for outdoor use, the woven seat is quite comfortable, requiring no cushion.*

FACING RIGHT: *Prior to garden furniture, our forebears took their indoor furniture outdoors for places to sit while enjoying the garden. Today, the carved wood dining chair has* been transformed into cast aluminum with a hand-applied antique finish. The weatherproof chair cushion is covered in a jacquard fabric that is an acrylic/polyester blend.

LEFT: *Reminiscent of the seating used in a nineteenth-century Parisian bistro, this cast-aluminum chair features a lattice back. The stylish box double-welt seat cushion is covered in a weather-resistant fabric.*

FACING: *Though it looks like fine wood, this Windsor chair is made of solid cast aluminum. It is a substantial chair that will not be moved by high winds. The design was inspired by a chair from George and Martha Washington's estate home. The seat pad is covered in outdoor acrylic fabric.*

LEFT: *Mount Vernon, the Virginia estate of George and Martha Washington, also provided the inspiration for this outdoor chair. Constructed of cast and extruded aluminum and shown in an antique white finish, the armchair is a replica of a mahogany chair in the home's dining room. The design of the beige and white tapestry cushion fabric, called Martha's Garden, was taken from wallpaper that lined a trunk belonging to Mrs. Washington.*

Aluminum

Due to its versatility, aluminum may be the most important material used for outdoor furniture today. It is lightweight, durable and rust-free. In order to capture intricate detail, aluminum may be cast using molds. Wrought aluminum uses a tube shaped from extruded aluminum. Whether cast or wrought, the furniture is usually covered with a weather-resistant, powder-coated finish that resists chipping and fading. A powder coat is a baked-on finish that forms a skin that bonds to the metal and is six times thicker than paint.

Black wrought iron has long been associated with outdoor furniture. Today, the look is still available but in the more user-friendly cast aluminum, which is not as heavy and will not rust. Lattice tabletops such as the one on the facing page and pages 30–31, are increasingly preferred over glass for their durability.

Brown and black are most often thought of as neutral colors for the outdoor room. However, gray is also a good choice for furniture frames and cushions. An outdoor room should blend with the natural setting, rather than compete. This collection demonstrates the many seating options available in outdoor furniture. Gather your friends for conversation, using the comfortable lounge chairs with the sofa or with a round coffee table large enough for beverages and hors d'oeuvres. Or relax poolside in the cast-aluminum sun chaise with its plush cushion covered in acrylic all-weather fabric. The dining table with umbrella provides another spot for easy entertaining.

Today's outdoor fabrics are functional and fashionable. Using the black and white palette of the floor tile, this cast-aluminum furniture features box double-welt cushions covered in an outdoor fabric with dots. The design on the back of the seating is reminiscent of lattice used in the garden for climbing vines. On pages 36–37, the lattice planter continues the theme.

Warm, natural browns continue to be favorite colors for outdoor furniture, particularly when used in conjunction with an inviting turquoise pool. The group on this page includes plush cushions that invite relaxation.

Large polka dot fabric adds pizzazz and is best used for accent pieces such as an umbrella cover and pillows. By choosing a solid neutral fabric for the furniture cushions, the look of an outdoor room can be quickly updated and changed, much in the same way that a change of jewelry can alter the look of a black dress.

FACING: A veranda or loggia lends itself to easy entertaining. In this handsome setting, the cast aluminum dining group includes a glass top table with comfortable chairs. Glass tops are better suited to covered areas rather than direct outdoor use, and add a more formal touch to the table. The urns with palms bring a touch of the garden inside.

LEFT: Cast aluminum is a material suitable for intricate designs. This handsome dining chair features an elaborately designed back with scrolled arms. The table mirrors the intricate design in its top and base.

Furniture is the mainstay of the outdoor room. In this case, the furniture closely resembles fine wood furniture you would expect to find indoors. Each piece has been hand sanded, painted and rubbed to create a pecan finish. The plush cushions and pillows are covered in an outdoor acrylic fabric that endures the elements. Add the handsome outdoor rug and floor lamp to create a living room outside as inviting as the one inside.

A broad sophisticated range of outdoor fabrics—with coordinating cords and trims—is now available in the marketplace. The furniture shown here is the same as the furniture shown on the previous two pages. However, the finishes (sandstone vs. chestnut

brown) and fabrics differ. Each color palette dramatically changes the look and mood. The weather-resistant cushions are trimmed in twisted cord welts.

Devotees of classic French country style can now have that look outdoors. This comfortable seating features gracefully curved ladderbacks, cast floral motifs, cabriole legs and woven seats. Handsome enough for use in any room in the home, the furniture is crafted of cast aluminum with a deluxe dark brown finish that resembles wood. The plush tailored cushions are covered in Sunbrella fabrics, including an attractive floral pattern as well as a neutral solid. Basketweave insets on the tables add charm to the setting.

Comfortable and stylish, this wicker furniture with wide arms is constructed of UV-resistant woven vinyl with powder-coated, welded aluminum frames. The scale of the sofa and chairs offer the same seating comfort of upholstered indoor furniture. Modern materials permit designs such as the double chaise with reclining dual backs that were previously unavailable. The fabrics are resistant to fading, spills and mildew.

Wicker

Beginning with the Victorian period, wicker furniture has been associated with porches and gardens. Originally, wicker was woven from rattan, willow or bamboo. These natural materials are durable enough to withstand sheltered outdoor use but do not fare well if exposed to harsh weather. Today, excellent synthetic materials, such as extruded resin or vinyl, are available that are totally weatherproof. Moreover, they are difficult to differentiate from wicker that is made from organic plant material. Wicker furniture made with new modern materials no longer needs to be sheltered under a roof, but can be exposed directly to sun and moisture.

An outdoor room with fireplace is an inviting spot for this handsome all-weather wicker collection. The mother/child chair (also called a chair and a half) is often used by adults with their pets. The outdoor lamps extend the room's use, and the rug adds warmth to the setting. Shown in an adjacent outdoor area, the cast-aluminum dining table is hand finished to look like wood.

Designed to enhance any sheltered outdoor room, this wicker collection is based on a process used in the United States for more than a hundred years. The woven wicker (composed of a paper product) is produced on a loom and sealed with a latex coating. Skilled craftspeople upholster

the wicker onto aluminum frames. A polyester paint finish adds color and durability. Designer acrylic fabrics and trims add to the style of the collection, while the rug and lamp complete the room.

Reminiscent of yester-year, this all-weather vinyl wicker has all the style and feel of natural wicker furniture, yet is far more durable. The wicker is hand woven and wrapped over heavy-gauge aluminum frames with stainless steel fittings. The 100 percent acrylic designer fabrics are sun- and water-resistant. The serving cart includes a handy removable serving tray.

Those with spacious outdoor rooms will appreciate the flexibility and versatility of this top-of-the-line sectional seating. Adding sections into a multitude of configurations may expand seating. Each piece of the handsome dining group, as well as the sectional seating and sun chaise, is made of strong aluminum frames covered in woven wicker composed of multi-tone resin in an antique black finish. This furniture will stand up to the elements, while providing style and comfort. The cushions and pillows are covered in designer acrylic fabrics. The rug, lamps and other accessories make this outdoor room truly livable.

RIGHT: *Mahogany—a dense and expensive outdoor wood—is ideal for a high-gloss paint finish. This mahogany bench is the epitome of elegant English garden furniture. Gorgeous design themes inspired by Mother Nature—intricate "cobwebs" and pierced seashells—come together with elegant latticework that hint at the furniture's regal origins.* **FACING:** *This is not your usual Adirondack design, and is evocative of Mackinac Island, Nantucket, White Sulphur Springs and other places associated with gracious summer living. Crafted of cypress, this furniture derives its whitewash look from a penetrating stain.*

Wood

Teak, meranti, cypress and mahogany are among the hardwoods suited for outdoor use. Unless painted or stained, these weather- and rot-resistant woods will age to a silvery gray. Adirondack-style furniture has long been associated with wood, as has the porch rocker, swing and glider. While painted mahogany outdoor furniture is elegant, it is also quite expensive. Teak furniture comes in many styles and in a broad range of prices; be sure to buy a brand you trust. Outdoor pieces made from furniture-grade woods such as oak and pine should be avoided unless used in a sheltered area and stored inside during the winter.

LEFT: *Crafted of meranti, a durable hardwood in the same family as mahogany, this handsome furniture is finished in a soft black with rubbed highlights. Meranti is a popular wood in Europe, where it is used for high quality joinery products such as facades and doors. The weather-resistant acrylic fabrics feature herringbone and leaf patterns. The outdoor rug with black border ties the setting together.*

BELOW: *Teak is an outdoor wood widely available in the marketplace. Quality varies so look for the highest grade of teak (Tectona grandis). Over time, teak will naturally weather from golden brown to a silver grey color. This premium teak modular deep seating allows for whatever size sofa and seating arrangement desired by connecting modules. The sturdy high back rocker is generous in size. The circular market umbrella—with a single-piece laminated teak pole for strength—comes with solid brass fittings.*

Based on historical French design, this wrought iron furniture is handcrafted in the United States using an anvil and hammer to forge intricate iron details. It was dipped into a bath of zinc phosphates and then electronically coated to create a permanent seal that locks out rust. A high quality powder-coat paint finish adds beauty and durability. The cushions are covered in Sunbrella fabric.

Wrought Iron

A nineteenth-century innovation, wrought iron became popular in outdoor furniture because of its look, its durability and its ability to resist the wind due to its weight. Bending hot steel rods on rigs by hand creates the pleasing curves and scrolls seen in much wrought-iron furniture. Period wrought-iron furniture was crafted of pure metal and rusted less than it does now. Unless it is hot-dip galvanized, wrought-iron furniture today—even with a durable powder-coat finish—will eventually develop rust and will need to be repainted. This is a small price to pay, if you desire the distinctive contours and style found in wrought iron.

Synthetic Materials

Today, resin or plastic furniture can look like wood, never needs painting and tolerates harsh seaside conditions. EnviroWood is a material made from recycled plastic bottles that are per-

meated with UV-stabilized coloring. It comes with a twenty-year warranty and is quite heavy. EnviroWood is a good choice for furniture in settings where strong winds and salty air prevail.

Crafted of EnviroWood, this white furniture will not turn yellow nor will it split. A nautical blue outdoor fabric is used for the comfortable cushions and umbrella cover. The accent pillows with dots, circles and stripes bring fun and life to the setting.

Handcrafted from select Italian marble and travertine, this all-weather table top is made in the United States by skilled artisans. The sturdy base is made of reinforced crushed stone. Based on a design found at the Clingencourt Antique Market in Paris, the stylish aluminum chairs are upholstered in an all-weather fabric with a contrasting welt.

Other Materials

There is almost an unlimited range of materials to choose from: cast iron (frequently found in antique benches); mosaic and stone-top tables; granite or cast-stone benches; and hammocks crafted of outdoor fabrics. Combining materials creates interest, as in pairing a stone table with aluminum chairs or using a chair made of metal and wood.

As long as weather permits, indoor furniture—a treasured antique rattan chair or an ottoman in a floral fabric, for example—can add pizzazz to the outdoor setting. Just remember to return them inside, when the day is done.

Toss a few pillows on a nearby bench or sofa and suddenly you have an inviting and cozy spot for conversation or a nap.

Torches or candle stakes can ensure safe passage to the outdoor room by lighting the path.

Candles must surely offer the most romantic lighting, whether indoors or outside.

Adorn the walls of outdoor rooms with eye-level art. Stylish wall décor is frequently crafted of weatherproof fiberglass or aluminum.

Plants are essential to the outdoor room, and containers are the ultimate accessory.

When it comes to style, details count—those individual decorations that express your personality and personalize an outdoor room.

CHAPTER 2

Accessorizing the Outdoor Room

Outdoor rooms can be stylish while reflecting your own personality. Plush pillows and throws, rugs, romantic lighting, and eye-catching wall décor are all available for outdoor use. Bring the garden directly into the outdoor room by using unique containers filled with blooming plants. Your selection of accents and accessories will make your room truly your own.

Celebrating
Your Own Style

Accessories provide an opportunity to put a personal stamp on your outdoor room. Celebrate your own style with accessories that make your outdoor area an inviting destination for family and friends. Surprisingly flexible, many outdoor accessories often grace the interior as a means of bringing the garden inside.

Fabrics

Furniture comes alive when colorful and imaginative outdoor fabrics are used for cushions, pillows, throws and umbrella covers. Made from fade-resistant, UV-stabilized fibers, the new outdoor fabrics are soft and weather-resistant. Moreover, the colors and designs bring beauty only previously associated with indoor décor.

Today, outdoor fabrics are being used indoors because they resist stains and tolerate the wear and tear of daily living. Furthermore, a sun-drenched room does not diminish their vibrant colors.

Most outdoor fabrics are made of acrylic, polyester or

a combination of synthetic fibers. All-weather trims and fringes are also available and add panache to cushions, pillows and throws. If the pillows or cushions become wet, just shake and let dry. The fibers used for the forms have been much improved; they resist mildew and the moisture passes through. Occasional rainfall can actually clean outdoor fabrics and furniture.

Toss a few pillows on a nearby bench or sofa and suddenly you have an inviting and cozy spot for conversation or a nap. Cuddle up with a book and a throw and drift into another dimension.

Rugs

Who could imagine a few years ago that rugs would be weatherproof? Beautiful outside or inside, the rugs are crafted of 100 percent olefin, which is weather-, fade- and mildew-resistant. A plethora of colors and designs are now available. Spills wipe away with a damp cloth.

A handsome rug is an easy way to define an outdoor room and soften a hardscape floor. It can pull furniture and accessories together while adding warmth and interest.

Add interest to an outdoor room with interesting pillows and cozy throws made from weather-resistant acrylic or polyester fabrics and trims. Consider changing your textile accessories seasonally to create an affordable new look. A wide array of fabric colors, textures and patterns is available in the marketplace.

Lighting

Extend enjoyment of the garden room into the evening hours by the creative use of lighting. Whether you choose electric light, candles or oil lamps, the ambience of the garden room is enhanced and its use prolonged for as many hours as you choose.

A good table or floor lamp is essential for reading. Look for lamps that are UV-listed as "suitable for wet locations," your assurance that the lamp is safe for out-

door use. Lamps constructed for use outside are often made of metal with a powder-coat finish or of a polymer material. The shade frames need to be covered in an outdoor fabric such as Sunbrella. Electric wall and ceiling fixtures, including chandeliers, can add a decorative touch while providing extra light.

Candles must surely offer the most romantic lighting, whether indoors or outside. Create warmth and intimacy by adding soft candlelight with candelabras, lanterns, hurricanes and sconces. Remember, flames may need to be protected from the breezes, so choose holders accordingly.

Torches or candle stakes can ensure safe passage to the outdoor room by lighting the path. Use citronella oil or citronella candles to help keep pesky insects away.

Light a path or define the parameter of your outdoor room with durable torches made of weather-tight, die-cast aluminum. Simply fill the canister with lamp oil and light the fiberglass wick. Only the oil burns away, not the wick.

Wall Décor

Adorn the walls of outdoor rooms with eye-level art. Planters busting with blooms, iron gates, or architectural elements bring dimension, color and interest. Salvage yards and flea markets are good sources of antique pieces. Stylish wall décor is frequently crafted of weather-proof fiberglass or aluminum. An outdoor clock/weather station can be functional and fun. Oftentimes, outdoor wall art is equally appealing inside the home.

FACING: *Transform an empty wall with this rustic brown iron and tole wall planter with hand-painted gold highlights. Pots of color may be added to the 6-inch-wide tray.*
RIGHT: *A replica of a historic garden gate, this hand-forged black grille adds interest wherever placed.*
BELOW: *Real slate is used to frame this handsome outdoor clock and weather station. It includes a thermometer and hygrometer.*

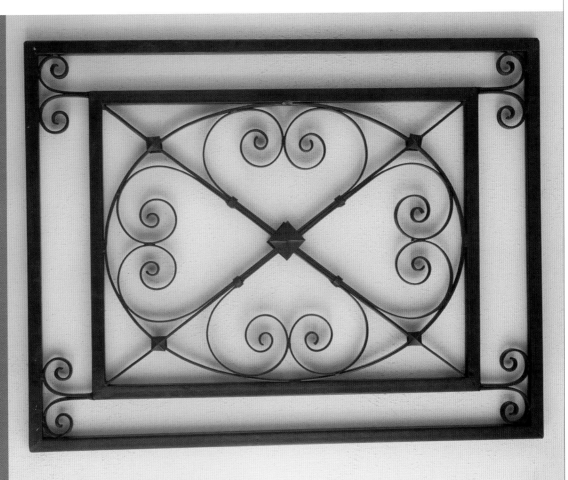

Shown with potted narcissus, this wall shelf also provides an ideal spot for small statues. Made of resin with a finish that resembles natural stone, it will endure variable weather.

ABOVE LEFT: *Shown with moss and jasmine, the Wentworth planter is crafted of iron with a black finish. It functions as wall art as well as a planter.*

LEFT: *With the appearance of aged stone, the Shell Planter is made from a mixture of sand and stones reinforced with a fiberglass backing. It is filled with oregano.*

ABOVE: *The Rising Sun plaque provides a fun focal point. Lightweight and easy to mount, it is cast from aluminum.*

BELOW LEFT: *With the appearance of aged stone, this container is crafted from a mixture of sand and stones cast into a surface using terrazzo-like techniques. The surface is then sandblasted and chemically treated. It is reinforced with a fiberglass backing. Lightweight yet durable, it may be left outdoors indefinitely.*

BELOW RIGHT: *This beautiful lady looks as if she might have lived during the seventeenth century. Crafted of resin to tolerate variable weather, the planter holds a standard 6-inch-diameter pot filled with flowers.*

FACING: *Inspired by French topiary forms, the birdbath planter is crafted of moss and chicken wire over a sturdy frame.*

Containers

Plants are essential to the outdoor room, and containers are the ultimate accessory. A pair of urns brings prominence to the entry of an outdoor room or, for that matter, the home's foyer. Plants in pots—massed in groups—add color and fragrance. Climbers may be restricted to a trellis or allowed to freely climb walls. Hanging baskets and wall planters expand the possibilities.

The container itself gives architectural form—structure—to your plant or tree. It allows you to put the plants and color exactly where you want them. Some planters are also works of art and come in almost any design or shape. The range of materials used to make containers is as varied as their styles: fiberglass, cast aluminum, wrought iron, cast stone, copper, iron, resin, wood, terra-cotta and more.

In selecting a container, consider your climate. Fiberglass and metal are frostproof, while only the finest terra-cotta won't crack when the temperature plummets.

FACING: *Planters of cast aluminum handsomely frame entries or provide focal points in the garden room. The urn on base is both sculpture and planter.*

ABOVE: *Resembling the traditional English trough, this simple container is made from a special mix of concrete and organic materials. The rough-hewn surface of the reproduction promotes the growth of moss to enhance the sense of age.*

RIGHT: *The Corinthian Planter borrows its design from classical architecture. It is made from a mixture of sand and stones with a fiberglass backing.*

Other Accents

When it comes to style, details count—those individual decorations that express your personality and communicate with your family and friends. Signs of welcome, watering cans, garden stakes, vases filled with cut flowers, wire baskets, antique garden tools—all are examples of objects that personalize an outdoor room.

Nothing is Written In Stone

Welcome to Our Garden
Please walk on the grass, smell the roses, hug the trees, talk to the birds, sit on the benches, and picnic on the lawn.

PEACE & GRACE
BE UNTO
THIS PLACE

FACING LEFT: *Change is inevitable. Adaptability is essential. This natural stone's etched message may resonate with you.*
FACING RIGHT: *Credit for the verbiage in this sign must be given to the Sydney, Australia Botanical Garden. This version is made of recycled wood and vinyl letters.*
ABOVE: *Made of slate with gold lettering, the sign is a* reminder of the tranquility an outdoor room can provide.
RIGHT: *Share the wisdom with those who visit your outdoor room. The sign is made of rust-free cast aluminum.*
BELOW: *Welcome guests to your garden or outdoor room with this sign crafted of grey slate with engraved letters painted black.*

Our garden gate
doth open wide
for all our friends
to walk inside.

Benches can be sculpture or a decorative element
that guides the eye and body to a contemplative spot.

Stone and terra-cotta to bronze and cast iron, antique and
new garden statuary have gained wide popularity in recent years.

This weather-durable sculpture is wonderful in the
garden or on a table in an outdoor room.

This charming wall fountain with a verdi and bronze finish is completely frost-proof. It is made of fiberglass with resin.

No matter the size of the outdoor room, find a spot for the soothing sound of water.

Antique reproductions of architectural fragments are an attractive and affordable alternative to the prohibitive costs of originals.

CHAPTER 3

Creating Visual Impact with Features

Every outdoor room needs the visual impact of art. Statuary and sculpture are particularly suited for outdoor use. Fountains evoke the senses through both form and sound. A beautiful bench draws the eye to the end of a vista while inviting a moment of quiet contemplation.

Art in the Garden

A feature—or focal point—is an important design element of an outdoor room. A means for adding visual impact, it can be as simple as a sundial or as grand as a stone fountain. Some features are integral to the outdoor room; others may be objets d'art at the end of a vista, viewed from a comfortable seat. Whatever the choice, the feature should complement nature.

LEFT: *With an intricately carved back and gracefully turned legs, this teak bench is stylish and comfortable. The gold and red tone pillows add panache.*
FACING: *The original "Fern and Blackberry" design (1858) has been traced to the English foundry, Coalbrookdale. This cast-aluminum reproduction in a lead patina finish is almost identical. The original cast-iron version is quite heavy and may be found occasionally at auction or in fine antique stores.*
FACING BELOW: *Made in England, this hand-wrought iron bench is almost eight feet long, providing a dramatic focal point in the garden. With its wonderful over-scrolled arms, the bench seats four and has been galvanized to stop rust forever.*

Benches as Art

Benches are nearly always more than seating. They can be sculpture or a decorative element that guides the eye and body to a contemplative spot. Benches come in myriad styles and are made of varied materials such as rustic faux bois, English-estate painted mahogany, Regency wrought iron, classic polished stone and Victorian wirework.

The English foundry, Coalbrookdale, made a wide array of iron benches in the nineteenth century, including "Fern and Blackberry." The firm's designs are emulated today in cast aluminum, a material that is easier to move.

Whether you find an antique bench at auction or opt for a reproduction of the seat, the design you choose will reflect the overall feeling you want to create in your outdoor room.

FACING: *Fashioned from a design from the Duchess of Devonshire's estate, Chatsworth, this mahogany bench is an example of elegant English garden furniture. It has been finished in a highly weather-resistant epoxy paint adapted from twenty-first-century technology and used to coat yacht hulls.*

LEFT: *This hand-carved granite bench with polished top will last a lifetime. It weighs 264 pounds and withstands high winds and the worst weather.*

Statuary, Sculpture & Ornaments

Throughout history, hand-carved stone statuary has been associated with elite gardens. Whether at Versailles or in the gardens of a vast English estate, statuary has assumed a dominant place.

Crafted in a variety of materials ranging from cast stone and terra-cotta to bronze and cast iron, antique and new garden statuary have gained wide popularity in recent years. The unique design and historic cachet of antique statues make them very appealing. Architectural

elements, such as columns and capitals, are in equal demand. The drawbacks in acquiring pieces of antiquity, however, are their availability, which tends to be scarce, and their cost, which tends to be prohibitive.

Antique reproductions of cherubs, nymphs or architectural fragments are an attractive and affordable alternative. Rather than imitate antiques, modern sculpture is also available. Often these artworks are made of fiberglass or fiber-reinforced cement. Whether figurative or abstract, statuary and sculpture should enhance rather than compete with the beauty of the outdoor room.

For a more informal setting, consider a decorative trellis covered in climbing roses or vines, a folk art piece, a gazing ball, an armillary, granite mushrooms or an aged staddle stone evocative of the English countryside. Whatever the well-placed artifact, it helps make an outdoor room truly your own.

ABOVE LEFT: *Beneath caladium leaves or bedded among small flowers, a set of four polished granite mushrooms adds interest and charm.*
LEFT and FACING: *With the appearance of aged stone, these ornaments are crafted from a mixture of sand and stones cast into a surface using terrazzo-like techniques. The surface is then sandblasted and chemically treated. Each is reinforced with a fiberglass backing. Lightweight yet durable, the ornaments may be left outdoors indefinitely.*

RIGHT: *Beauty and grace describe this classic figure named for Queen Charlotte. It is hand cast in fiber-reinforced concrete, a pecan wash adds an aged look. This weather-durable sculpture is wonderful in the garden or on a table in an outdoor room.*

ABOVE: *Acorn finial.*
ABOVE RIGHT: *Add height and structure to a container or garden bed with this handsome pillar. It is crafted of iron with a charcoal brown powder-coat finish.*
RIGHT: *This cottage exudes old world charm with its textured aged surfaces. Made by artisans in the United States, it is hand cast using a fiber-reinforced concrete that endures virtually any climate. This ornament has a removable roof for a secret hiding place.*

LEFT: *Handcarved in rose granite, the millstone fountain creates a soothing, contemplative atmosphere in the garden. The millstone rests on a round rose granite stone; together, they weigh about 600 pounds.*

ABOVE: *These solid brass cranes with verdigris finish add beauty to the garden while providing a soothing sound. A "T-off" enables both cranes to run off one pump (170 gallons per hour).*

Fountains, A Sensual Delight

No matter the size of the outdoor room, find a spot for the soothing sound of water. Fountains, whether confined to a small tabletop or expansive as a two-tiered extravaganza, provide tranquility and calm.

Stone fountains, while luxurious, can be prohibitively expensive. A good alternative material is fiberglass, or glass-fiber-reinforced cement, which resembles stone and withstands harsh temperatures. Brass, aluminum,

cast iron and cast stone are other possibilities. Whatever the choice of material, there are many beautifully crafted styles—wall and freestanding—available to capture the mood you envision.

Fountains operate by recycling water in their basin or pool. The flow of water from a fountain depends on the velocity of the pump (GPH, gallons per hour). Pumps are submersible, available in many sizes and inexpensive to operate. The key is to maintain an adequate level of water so the pump does not burn out. Many homeowners regularly refill their fountains with a garden hose; others use a plumbing device that automatically turns water on when the level drops. For evening enchantment, be sure your water feature is lit.

FACING: *Crafted of fiberglass with resin and crushed stone, this fountain is durable and weather-resistant (to -10 degrees F). The Roman finish is incorporated in the molding process, ensuring lasting beauty. To use the fountain, fill the basin with water from a hose and turn on the pump.*

ABOVE LEFT: *A pineapple adorns the top of this extraordinary two-tier fountain. The aged stone finish is incorporated in the molding process, ensuring lasting beauty. It's made of fiberglass with crushed stone.*

ABOVE: *This charming wall fountain with a verdi and bronze finish is completely frost-proof. It is made of fiberglass with resin.*

LEFT: *Classic in design, the handsome lion fountain is crafted of reconstituted stone that has been reinforced with fiberglass for strength. A permanent stain provides a patina of age.*

A birdbath not only attracts birds but also serves as a lovely ornament.

While a sanctuary, an outdoor room is also a place for laughter, fun and whimsy.

Why not furnish an outdoor room using children's furniture?

Children love this solid bronze fountain featuring a
boy squeezing his pet frog.

Crafted from glass-fiber-reinforced cement, this birdbath features a child
trying to peek inside the bowl, perhaps to glimpse a bird bathing.

Even the most formal outdoor room benefits
from a touch of humor.

CHAPTER 4

Bringing the
Outdoor Room
Alive

A lifetime of memories can be
created outside. Here is a place
where family and friends gather
to enjoy games, conversation
and meals. Children love the
expansiveness and freedom of
outdoor rooms where they can
play and enjoy an ice cream
cone without the fear of drops
on the furniture or rug. Humor
and whimsy in outdoor accents
add to the enjoyment, as does
the sway of a glider or swing.

Enjoying the
Outdoor Lifestyle

A beautifully furnished outdoor room is an extension of the house. It becomes a part of the home when it is filled with the sounds of life. Bring it alive through humor, songbirds, games, and the pleasures of alfresco dining. Today, family and guests gather outdoors where there are natural light, unlimited ceilings, and gardens that delight the senses.

RIGHT: *Crafted from glass-fiber-reinforced cement, this birdbath features a child trying to peek inside the bowl, perhaps to glimpse a bird bathing.*

FACING ABOVE: *Crafted from glass-fiber-reinforced cement, this bird sculpture also has a basin for water (hidden behind the wing) so it may function as a birdbath. The weight is approximately one-third what the same sculpture would weigh if cast in stone. The sculpture endures temperature change and requires no maintenance. Its aged bronze finish will develop a distinctive patina over time.*

FACING BELOW: *With the appearance of aged stone, the cherubs birdbath is crafted from a mixture of sand and stones cast into a surface using terrazzo-like techniques. The surface is then sandblasted and chemically treated (variations in color will occur). It is reinforced with a fiberglass backing. Lightweight yet durable, this birdbath may be left outdoors indefinitely.*

Birds

Birds add joy to the outdoor room. Attract them with birdbaths, birdhouses and bird feeders. Be sure you select bird-related items that are functional as well as decorative.

Houses/feeders need to be constructed of outdoor wood such as cedar, cypress or mahogany or durable PVC boards. Houses and feeders with copper roofs tolerate the weather and will develop a patina with age.

Keep the entrance hole 1.5 inches in diameter, look for drainage holes in the bottom and be sure there is an access door for cleaning.

Birds need water in both summer and winter. A birdbath not only attracts birds but also serves as a lovely ornament. It may be made from almost any material. Aluminum and fiberglass are best in cold climates; a ceramic bath can crack when the water freezes. Birdbaths need to have sufficient water depth and require refilling if rainfall is insufficient.

Most varieties of garden birds have a great appetite for the pests that populate your garden. Give them a safe place to feed and bathe and they will return time and again. And by all means, don't forget to leave some food out.

LEFT: *Add a flight of fancy to a banister or fence post. The bird finial is crafted of resin to endure variable weather. It comes with a firmly embedded screw for easy installation.*
ABOVE: *An adaptation of an English dovecote, this eight-compartment house is handcrafted of cypress with cedar shingles.*
BELOW LEFT: *Over 4.5 inches high, the Martin Mansion with handsome lacquered copper roof has 12 perches. It is crafted of PVC board*

construction for dura-
bility and beauty. This
majestic house will
attract Purple Martins,
known for hearty mos-
quito appetites.
FACING BELOW RIGHT:
*This attractive feeder
with a copper roof in a
verdigris finish is made
of PVC board construc-
tion. Lift the roof off to
fill the Plexiglas tube
with seed.*
RIGHT: *This set of handcrafted, colorful, glazed
clay birds adds interest
and charm to a container
or flowerbed.*

Wit and Whimsy

While a sanctuary, an outdoor room is also a place for laughter, fun and whimsy. Objects can evoke a variety of feelings. A frog doing a handstand will bring smiles from passersby, and avid gardeners may chuckle when they see garden markers poking fun at Latin plant names. Even the most formal outdoor room benefits from a touch of humor.

FACING LEFT: *With proper watering and an occasional haircut, these live topiary bunnies will give pleasure throughout the growing season. Bring them inside when winter comes.*
FACING RIGHT: *Keep that unruly hose under control with this dancing frog hose guide made of brass and aluminum.*
ABOVE: *Toads love this stylish house. Crafted of hand-cast stone, the house protects them from predators and the hot sun.*

A garden's friend, each toad eats thousands of pesky insects.
RIGHT: *Crafted of solid brass with a verdigris finish, the frog on lily pad always brings a smile to passersby (as does the frog birdbath below.)*
BELOW RIGHT: *These stoneware garden markers are guaranteed to bring a chuckle to avid gardeners. The set includes Bloomis Notimus, Plantus Unknownus, Weedis Victorius and Costa Fortunii.*

Relaxation and Fun

Who can resist a swing hung from a porch ceiling or tree? And what can be more enjoyable than two friends whiling away the hours in a glider? Motion is a great way to relax.

How about an afternoon with a grandchild playing checkers, chess or cards? Have you thought about a dartboard on a garden room wall? Croquet and boules are lawn games that lend themselves to larger outdoor

spaces. Keep games and play materials handy in your garden room.

To surround yourself and guests with outdoor music, situate outdoor speakers above seating for good sound, and contain that sound so it does not disturb neighbors. Sound systems should be waterproof so they are safe from surges.

Children

Outdoor rooms are great places for children. They need space to play and use their imaginations. Why not furnish an outdoor room using children's furniture? Add accessories such as a colorful birdhouse or a fountain featuring a child squeezing a frog. Small animals cast from stone or metal add charm and enchantment. Or how about a butterfly house? Attract real creatures—such as squirrels and frogs—by providing water and a source of food such as nuts and berries.

FACING: *Children love this solid bronze fountain featuring a boy squeezing his pet frog. The sight and sound will give pleasure year-round.*

ABOVE: *Winged friends flutter in the slotted front of this cypress butterfly house. Trimmed in copper with copper butterflies, the celery-colored house adds interest to the garden for children and adults alike.*

RIGHT: *The appealing dog with basket may be left outdoors indefinitely. It is crafted from a mixture of sand and stones reinforced with fiberglass backing.*

FACING: *Suitable for use in a garden room as well as inside, this children's furniture is crafted in solid teak. Carving a child's name in serif letters on the back of the bench or a chair creates an heirloom gift.*

LEFT: *These children's teak steamer chairs are reproductions of the adult steamer chair once used on the Queen Mary. The comfy and colorful cushions are covered in an outdoor polyester fabric.*

ABOVE: *A desirable size for bluebirds and other small songbirds, this hand-painted birdhouse with bunny is made of cypress with a cedar-shingled roof trimmed with copper. The art is sprayed with a clear sealer for lasting beauty.*

RIGHT: *Enamelware is ideal for outdoor use since it is non-breakable. The cabbage motif adds charm to any alfresco setting.*
FACING LEFT: *For summer entertaining, terra cotta long tom pots—lined with parchment paper—are ideal for serving crudités.*
FACING RIGHT: *Double duty, a potting bench can be used for entertaining as well as potting plants and flowers.*
A hollowed-out watermelon is a great vase for flowers.

Alfresco Dining

Dining outdoors has a casualness and ease to it that is quite appealing. The food can be simple: crudités (perhaps served in terra-cotta long toms), salads and fruit, fish or meat grilled or barbequed with fresh herbs, and beverages such as lemonade, iced tea or a crisp wine.

Add a cloth to the table for special occasions. Decorating can be effortless by filling a vase with cut flowers and foliage from the garden. For an evening gathering, candles in hurricanes or lanterns bring night magic.

Sharing the Outdoor Room

Sharing a gracious outdoor room with loved ones is a great pleasure. It may be as easy as spending a quiet morning over coffee with a friend or as energizing as hosting a crowd for a holiday celebration. Whatever the activity, an outdoor room can be a source of lifetime memories.

A Large Marketplace

It has been less than two decades since outdoor fabrics were limited to solid colors such as forest green, navy or natural and a few striped or floral fabrics. Outdoor furniture and garden accessories were found at local "casual furniture" stores or garden centers. A few retail companies specializing in a full range of outdoor furnishings and accessories could be found in major cities.

Enter the baby boomers, who wholeheartedly embraced the garden lifestyle. Retailers and manufacturers alike listened to their wants and needs. The revolution in garden furnishings took root.

Local Resources

Garden centers, furniture dealers, "big box" stores, architectural salvage firms, antiques shops and garden shows are just a few of the local sources for garden furnishings. A review of the yellow pages and local newspaper advertising is a good way to identify sources within your own community.

As local venues increased, delivery services such as UPS and Federal Express expanded the possibilities by bringing furniture and accessories to the home from locations hundreds, even thousands, of miles away.

Catalog, Internet and Television Resources

Specialty catalogs such as Smith & Hawken, Horchow Garden and Charleston Gardens have been offering garden furnishings for more than a decade. Today, other home-oriented mail order catalogs such as Pottery Barn, Restoration Hardware and Source Perrier feature outdoor furnishings in their spring and summer offerings.

The emergence of the Internet has changed the marketplace forever. It is a powerful means for identifying and buying "just the right" outdoor furniture collection, water feature, antique statue or birdhouse. An almost limitless range of outdoor furnishings is available online. Some merchants are "net only," while others are "multi-channel," using the Internet, direct mail such as catalogs and "bricks and mortar" stores to market their offerings.

Cable and satellite television present a broad range of home-focused programs that include ideas and sources for furnishing garden rooms. Garden-related magazines are another good source of design ideas and product leads.

From Scarcity to Plenty

The days of scarce offerings from few sources are over. Now, more than ever, it is important to buy brands you trust from retailers with proven track records. Always look for a guarantee that allows you to return your purchase, for any reason whatsoever, within a reasonable period of time. Repeat business is what keeps companies going for the long-term, so the reliable retailers stand behind their products.

If you know a design professional, seek his or her advice about where and what to buy. When you admire furnishings in a friend's garden room, ask about her experience. Above all, enjoy the process of putting together an outdoor room that reflects your own style and way of life.

Mail Order Catalog/Internet Companies with Outdoor Furnishings

Charleston Gardens®
www.charlestongardens.com

Crate & Barrel
www.crateandbarrel.com

Frontgate
www.frontgate.com

Horchow Garden
www.horchow.com

Pottery Barn
www.potterybarn.com

Restoration Hardware
www.restorationhardware.com

Smith & Hawken
www.smithandhawken.com

Source Perrier
www.sourceperrier.com

Outdoor Furniture Manufacturers with Dealer Networks

Barlow Tyrie
www.teak.com
Classic teak furniture; some designs with stainless steel and aluminum accents.

Gloster
www.gloster.com
Stylish teak furniture.

Kingsley-Bate
www.kingsleybate.com
Teak furniture and umbrellas.

Lloyd Flanders
www.lloydflanders.com
Loom and all-weather wicker furniture.

New River Furniture
www.newriverfurniture.com
Brazilian cherry porch furniture.

O.W. Lee
www.owlee.com
Wrought-iron furniture made in the United States.

Pride Family Brands
www.prideoutdoor.com
Stylish cast- and tubular-aluminum furniture.

Riverwood Casual
www.riverwoodcasual.com
Cypress Adirondack furniture.

Rock Wood Furniture
www.rockwoodteak.com
Teak furniture and garden accessories.

Seaside Casual
www.seasidecasual.com
EnviroWood furniture comes with 20-year warranty.

Summer Classics
www.summerclassics.com
Broad selection of aluminum, all-weather wicker, wrought-iron, and teak furniture.

Terra Furniture
www.terrafurniture.com
Aluminum, teak and wood furniture featuring classic styles.

Uwharrie Chair
www.uwharriechair.com
Rustically styled pine furniture.

Veneman Furniture
www.venemanfurniture.com
Contemporary aluminum, wicker
and wood furniture.

Whitecraft
www.whitecraft.net
Wicker and rattan collections.

Windham Furniture
www.windhamcastings.com
Cast-aluminum furniture made
in the United States.

Woodard Furniture
www.woodard-furniture.com
Cast- and tubular-aluminum and
wicker furniture collections and
accessories.

Garden Accessories and Containers

Accents of France
www.accentsoffrance.com
Decorative treillage.

Campo de' Fiori
www.campodefiori.com
Moss-covered terra-cotta pots
and accents; iron and copper
architectural objects.

Haddonstone
www.haddonstone.com
Cast-stone containers, ornaments
and architectural elements.

Tuscan Imports
www.tuscanimports.com
Terra-cotta containers and accents
from Impruneta and Siena.

Lamp Manufacturers with Dealer Networks

Olympia Lighting Products
www.olympialighting.com
Outdoor lamps, chandeliers and
fixtures.

Shady Lady
www.shadyladylighting.com
Large assortment of outdoor lamps.

Outdoor Rugs with Dealer Networks

Capel Rugs
www.capelrugs.com
Capel Anywhere rugs are for use
inside and outside.

Couristan
www.couristan.com
Polypropylene rugs for outdoor living.

Trans-Ocean Import
www.transocean.com
Contemporary and classic designs
crafted of polypropylene.

Textile Manufacturers

ESP Elaine Smith Pillows
www.elainesmithdesigns.com
Decorative outdoor pillows and
throws.

Glen Raven Custom Fabrics
www.sunbrella.com
Broad range of outdoor fabrics
in solids and jacquards.

Laurie Bell
www.lauriebell.com
Outdoor pillows, floor cushions
and ottomans.